NEW JERSEY

The Garden State

★

TEN TOP FACTS ABOUT NEW JERSEY

★ ★ ★ ★ ★ ★ ★ ★ ★ ★ ★ ★ ★

•State nicknames:	The Garden State, The Land of Provisions
•State motto:	Liberty and Prosperity
•Capital:	Trenton
•Area:	7,787 square miles
•State flower:	Violet
•State tree:	Red oak
•State bird:	Eastern goldfinch
•State insect:	Honeybee
•State dinosaur:	Hadrosaur
•State shell:	Knobbed whelk (conch shell)

D1411988

For Robert, Brendan, and Emmett Maloney

——— THE ———
Jim Henson
—COMPANY—

12 11 10 9 8 7 6 5 4 3 2 1   0 1 2 3 4 5/0

Designed by Madalina Stefan

Printed in the U.S.A.

First Scholastic printing, November 2000

NEW JERSEY
The Garden State

By Suzanne Weyn

SCHOLASTIC INC.
New York Toronto London Auckland Sydney Mexico City New Delhi Hong Kong

A Celebration of the Fifty States

★ ★ ★ ★ ★ ★ ★ ★ ★ ★ ★ ★ ★

In January 1999, the U.S. Mint started an ambitious ten-year program to commemorate each of the fifty United States. Over the next several years (through 2008), they will issue five newly designed quarters each year.

One side (obverse) of each new quarter will display the profile of George Washington and the words Liberty, In God We Trust, *and* United States of America. *The other side (reverse) will feature a design honoring a specific state's unique history, the year it became a state, the year of the quarter's issue, and the words* E Pluribus Unum (*Latin for "from many, one"*). *The quarters are being issued in the order in which the states joined the union, beginning with the thirteen original colonies.*

To find out more about the 50 State Quarters™ Program, visit the official U.S. Mint Web site at www.usmint.gov.

NEW JERSEY'S QUARTER:
Crossroads of the Revolution

When you look on the back of a New Jersey quarter you see a picture of George Washington standing in a boat with other members of the colonial army. They are crossing the Delaware River on their way to a surprise attack against the British in Trenton on Christmas night in 1776.

The words *Crossroads of the Revolution* are printed below the picture because nearly one hundred battles took place in New Jersey during the Revolutionary War. Washington's two major defeats of the British in Trenton and in Princeton gave the colonists a military advantage that helped them win independence from England.

The quarter's design is based on "Washington Crossing the Delaware," a painting done in 1851 by the artist Emanuel Leutze. The original painting hangs in the Metropolitan Museum of Art in New York City.

The First Settlers

The land now known as New Jersey was inhabited by the Lenni Lenape Indians for ten thousand years before any European set foot on its shores. (The name Lenni Lenape means "original people.") The Powhatan-Renape tribe also lived there.

Giovanni da Verrazano, from Florence, Italy, was the first European to see New Jersey. He sailed along the Jersey coast and anchored off Sandy Hook in 1524.

His exploration didn't inspire any European settlement at the time. It wasn't until 1609 that another European, Henry Hudson, arrived in a ship called *the Half Moon*. Hudson was English, but he and his sailors worked for a Dutch-owned company.

Giovanni da Verrazano

Dutch adventurers, fur trappers, and traders followed. By 1620, a trading post was set up in an area that is now part of Jersey City. Over the next fifteen years, several other Dutch colonies were settled.

The English, however, had never recognized Dutch claims to New Jersey. In 1664, the Dutch were forced to surrender their land to the English.

King Charles II of England granted the captured Dutch colony to his brother, James, Duke of York. The Duke of York, in turn, gave control of the land between the Delaware and Hudson Rivers (the Hudson River had been named for Henry Hudson) to Lord John Berkeley and Sir George Carteret. George Carteret then appointed his cousin, Philip Carteret, as the first colonial governor. It was Berkeley and Carteret who first called the land New Jersey, after the Isle of Jersey in the English Channel.

In 1674, Edward Billinge and John Fenwick, Quaker leaders, bought Lord John Berkeley's share of the colony. Quakers, who were experiencing religious persecution in England and other parts of Europe, flooded into the northeast area (including New York, New Jersey, Delaware, and Pennsylvania), drawn by its religious freedom.

By 1676, New Jersey was officially divided into West Jersey (controlled by William Penn) and East Jersey (controlled by Carteret). West Jersey was dominated by Quakers. East Jersey was controlled mostly by Scottish partners of the original proprietors of the land. In 1702, Queen Anne of England united East and West Jersey into a single royal colony.

The Duke of York

Philip Carteret

The Fight for Independence

Many of New Jersey's settlers began to grow restless under British rule. Along with other American colonists, they resented having to pay high taxes to England without receiving any representation in the British government in return. A movement to break away from England and become an independent nation began to gain popularity. By June 1775, the New Jersey Provincial Congress voted to form its own militia to aid the main Continental army in its fight for freedom.

There were people in New Jersey, however, who were *not* in favor of independence from England. Because of these Loyalists (colonists loyal to England), the English maintained a strong presence in New Jersey during the early days of the Revolutionary War. The English also hired soldiers from the German state of Hesse, called Hessians, who came to New Jersey and fought on their side.

Hessian troops

New Jersey's Minutemen

Minutemen were American men who could be ready to fight the British wherever they were needed at a minute's notice. New Jersey had its own brave Minutemen who helped General Washington and his Continental army win battles in New Jersey. Here are excerpts from the militia act passed by the New Jersey Provincial Congress in 1775:

"The Congress taking into consideration the cruel and arbitrary measures adopted by the British Parliament for the purpose of subjugating the American Colonies to the most abject servitude . . . do think it highly necessary that the inhabitants of this Province be forthwith properly armed and disciplined for the defense of the cause of American freedom. . . . That for the purpose of effectually carrying into execution the recommendation of the Continental Congress respecting the appointment of minute-men, four thousand able-bodied effective men be enlisted and enrolled who shall hold themselves in constant readiness, on the shortest notice, to march to any place where their assistance may be required for the defense of this or any neighboring colony."

"Washington Crossing the Delaware" by Emanuel Leutze

By 1776, the British seemed to be winning the war. The colonial troops were discouraged and hungry. The English had taken New York and forced General George Washington's troops to retreat across the Delaware River into Pennsylvania.

But on a bitter cold Christmas in 1776, Washington and his troops secretly returned to New Jersey across the Dela-ware River under the cover of darkness. (In the picture on the state quarter you can see ice floating in the river.)

Since it was a holiday, the Hessian troops in Trenton were caught off guard when the Continental army attacked in the early morning hours of December 26. Today you can tour Washington Crossing State Park in scenic Titusville and relive that historic day in 1776.

The Battle of Monmouth

Washington followed this win with another victory at the Battle of Princeton in 1777. These two defeats forced the British to retreat to New York, but they tried again and again to recapture New Jersey.

One of the most famous battles fought in New Jersey was the Battle of Monmouth. In 1778, the British army fled their encampment in Philadelphia and came through the town of Freehold in Monmouth County. The battle ended in a draw. Washington and his troops spent much of the next two years in New Jersey.

The Battle of Springfield in June 1780 finally swept the British from the state. After the British were defeated in 1783, Americans set out to build a new democratic nation. In 1787, New Jersey was the third state to ratify (meaning to accept) the U.S. Constitution, and in 1789, it was the first to ratify the Bill of Rights.

Trenton Makes, the World Takes

New Jersey's state motto is "Liberty and Prosperity" — well chosen in light of the years following the Revolutionary War. In 1790, Trenton was selected as the state capital, and became known the world over for its chinaware, ceramic pottery, steel, and rubber goods. The steel cables used to construct the George Washington Bridge, Golden Gate Bridge, and Brooklyn Bridge were made in Trenton.

In 1791, Alexander Hamilton — in his role as Secretary of the Treasury under President Washington — established the town of Paterson on the Passaic River as the site of a planned industrial city. The river's seventy-seven-foot-high waterfall, Great Falls, was one of the nation's first tourist attractions and a source of hydraulic power. Hamilton's planned town was a success. Paterson quickly became known for producing cotton and silk, machinery, and railroad locomotives.

Passaic River in Paterson

9

The state's location — between New York City and Philadelphia, and between New England and the South — created a need for more transportation. Throughout the 1800s, roads were built, canals dug, and railroads constructed. The first steam locomotive that actually pulled a train on a track was built by John Stevens of Hoboken in 1824.

In the second half of the 1800s, many of New Jersey's small towns became industrial centers. Farmers hoping to make a better living moved into the big cities, such as Newark, Jersey City, Paterson, Camden, and Trenton. By 1900, most of New Jersey's population of nearly half a million lived in the industrial northern part of the state.

Railroad sectioners at work

Laying the tracks

The Civil War — Soldiers and Solderers

In 1861, the Southern states wanted to become independent from the rest of America in order to protect their right to keep slaves. The South believed — correctly — that slavery would soon be outlawed in the United States.

The federal government in Washington, D.C., led by President Abraham Lincoln, didn't want the South to leave the union of states. This conflict resulted in the Civil War.

Tens of thousands of New Jersey soldiers fought on the side of the Northern states, also known as the Union. The Underground Railroad, a system that helped runaway slaves escape to the North, ran through the state as well.

The demand for supplies during the war kept New Jersey's factories and foundries booming. Railroad track mileage nearly doubled during this time.

Lincoln and his generals

The fast industrial growth brought about by the war continued in peacetime and the entire state prospered greatly in the late 1800s. Its expansion was partially due to the many inventors who lived in New Jersey who were responsible for a number of technological advances. The greatest genius in this group was Thomas Alva Edison, the inventor of the electric lightbulb and the phonograph, among other things.

Fugitives arriving at a station of the Underground Railroad

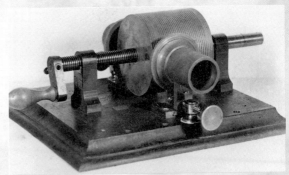

Thomas Edison's original tinfoil phonograph of 1877

Aerial view of Paterson, 1930

Industrial Growth

During World War I (1914–1918), New Jersey's industrial growth continued as its industrial centers provided much-needed supplies to the Allies. Oil refineries and ammunition plants were created to meet the U.S. and Allied demand for fuel and weaponry.

This boom in manufacturing suffered during the 1930s when all of America experienced the Great Depression. It was a time when the economies of many nations were in trouble, and jobs were hard to come by.

In 1939, World War II started, and the United States began supplying goods to European nations at war. New Jersey once again geared up to supply chemicals, textiles, munitions, and other military materials. Once the United States got involved in the war, New Jersey continued to contribute supplies. The state's shipyards constructed aircraft carriers and battleships and built nearly one-fourth of the destroyers used by the U.S. Navy during the war.

From the end of World War II in 1945 through the present, New Jersey has remained a vital industrial center.

New Jersey Today

Today New Jersey ranks first in the nation in chemical production, with items such as bulk chemicals and pharmaceuticals. Other goods manufactured include processed foods, brewed beverages, navigation equipment, surgical appliances, and photographic supplies. One of the most important minerals extracted in the state is basalt, used in construction. But with more than one hundred rivers and streams (1,400 miles of which is trout stream) and more than eight hundred lakes and ponds, New Jersey has plenty of natural beauty, too.

Kayaker on Great Egg Harbor River

The state is famous for its miles of sandy coastline (nearly 130 miles worth!), and seaside resort towns. Atlantic City is the home of the world's longest boardwalk, the famous Miss America Pageant, and the first modern gambling casinos outside of Nevada. (The street names in the original Monopoly game are taken from the street names in Atlantic City as well.) Today New Jersey ranks as the seventh most popular state for tourism.

Atlantic City in its early days

New Jersey shore today

13

The Garden State

New Jersey's rich lands and hearty soil were perfect for growing fruits and vegetables. Colonists described the area as a garden because of its agricultural bounty. And New Jersey's many seaports gave it easy access to the markets of Philadelphia and New York City. These cities received much of their produce from New Jersey, earning the state its nickname the Garden State.

Today, it is still well deserved — New Jersey has more than 8,000 farms, and it is a leading producer of cultivated blueberries, cranberries, peaches, eggplant, asparagus, bell peppers, fresh market spinach, lettuce, cucumbers, sweet corn, and fresh market tomatoes.

Some Famous Events in New Jersey's History

The Hindenburg Disaster

The U.S. Naval Air Station in Lakehurst was once "Blimp Central" for the world.

In 1919, the U.S. Navy bought the site in central New Jersey as a base for its lighter-than-air craft — airships, sometimes called blimps. In 1923, the first American-made airship, the *Shenandoah,* made its first flight from Lakehurst.

The Lakehurst airfield was also the starting and finishing point for the German *Graf Zeppelin's* twenty-one-day trip around the world in 1929.

The airships were hard to handle. When flying at low speeds and during their landing approach, they were practically impossible to steer. They were also subject to the whims of the wind and the weather. The airships of this era had to shed ballast at takeoff and release gas during landing. Ground crews of up to 250 people had to hold down the giant airships with ropes and moor them by hand.

Despite this, the airships grew in popularity. They were considered a luxurious way to cross the Atlantic.

Then, on May 6, 1937, a terrible disaster struck. An 840-foot-long luxury German airship called the *Hindenburg* was attempting to land in Lakehurst. Suddenly, the huge craft turned into a fireball just 249 feet above the ground!

Below, onlookers watched helplessly as passengers leaped from the flaming gondola on the underside of the ship. Thirty-five people onboard and one member of the ground crew died that day.

At the time, the fire was blamed on thunderstorms that had showered Lakehurst earlier in the day. Historians and airship experts believed that the electrically charged air sparked the hydrogen inside the balloon. More recently it has been suspected that the ship's cotton covering (treated with resin and aluminum) was flammable enough to have sparked and caused the fire.

This disaster ended the age of the airship's use for luxury travel.

The crash of the *Hindenburg*

Mars Attacks!

In 1938, on Halloween Eve, a radio broadcast of popular music was interrupted for an alarming announcement.

Grover Mills, a small town in New Jersey, had been invaded by Martians armed with ray guns!

People panicked. Some armed themselves. There were traffic jams all over as people in Grover Mills and neighboring towns tried to flee from the hostile aliens.

Was it real? No, it was just a radio play based on *The War of the Worlds,* a novel written by H.G. Wells. A young director, actor, and filmmaker named Orson Welles thought it would make a thrilling radio drama. In the beginning of the show, Welles had even announced that it was fictional. But not everyone heard the announcement and for several hours people believed the invasion was real. Some radio stations play this spooky broadcast every Halloween.

Deadly Duel

Before dawn one July day in 1804, two men — both famous American statesmen — faced each other in a duel on the shores of the Hudson River in the town of Weehawken. One was Vice President Aaron Burr. The other was former Secretary of the Treasury Alexander Hamilton.

Time and again, Hamilton refused to support Burr in his political campaigns. He had prevented him from becoming president of the United States, and later governor of New York. When Hamilton publicly called Burr a man who could not be trusted, Burr had had enough. He called for a duel.

The men paced off and shot. Hamilton fell to the ground, dead.

This duel ended Burr's political career, along with the life of Alexander Hamilton.

Face-off between Alexander Hamilton and Aaron Burr

Thomas Edison's home in West Orange

Eureka!

Thomas Alva Edison once said, "Genius is one percent inspiration, ninety-nine percent perspiration." Despite only three months of formal schooling, Edison *was* a genius and one of the most prolific inventors in history. Although born in Ohio in 1847, he spent most of his career as an inventor in New Jersey — first at his manufacturing plant in Newark, and then at his laboratories in Menlo Park and West Orange.

On October 21, 1879, Thomas Edison demonstrated his carbon-filament incandescent lamp, which burned for two days. He soon held a public demonstration, illuminating his Menlo Park laboratory complex with a circuit of thirty lamps, each of which could be turned on and off without affecting the rest. This event at his pilot light-and-power station marked the beginning of the electrical age.

Replica of Edison's original lightbulb

Hadrosaurus foulkii

Haddonfield is the birthplace of modern paleontology — the science of studying dinosaur fossils — thanks to the discovery of the first nearly complete skeleton of a dinosaur in 1858. Although bones had been studied in both Europe and North America prior to that date, this site contained enough bones from the same animal to prove that dinosaurs had really existed.

Things to Do and Places to See

Sunrise Mountain on the Appalachian Trail

Mansion in Cape May

The Appalachian Trail

Stretching from Georgia to Maine, the 2,160-mile-long Appalachian Trail passes through the Kittatinny Mountains and the highlands of New Jersey. More than 250 hikers travel it end to end each year. The trail is lush with wildlife and breathtaking views.

In New Jersey, the trail begins at the Delaware Water Gap, travels through High Point State Park (the highest spot in New Jersey, overlooking three states), and ends at the New York border of Greenwood Lake.

Delaware Water Gap

Cape May

The southernmost town on New Jersey's shore, the entire city of Cape May was designated a National Historic Landmark in 1976. Many of its homes and hotels date back to the end of the nineteenth century and are impressive examples of Victorian architecture.

Cape May is also the home of one of the most famous bird-watching locations in North America. Ornithologists (people who study birds) flock to the Cape May Bird Observatory, one of the busiest migratory bird stops on the planet. Over 700 different species have been spotted there.

Searching for Cape May "diamonds" is a popular family activity along the Jersey Cape, especially at Sunset Beach. These smooth shiny crystals are actually broken pieces of quartz found in the northern region of the Delaware River and washed ashore by the tides.

Great egret

Nassau Hall, Princeton University

Princeton University

Princeton, the fourth-oldest university in the United States, is one of the seven famous Ivy League schools. The university houses the Institute for Advanced Study, where German-born physicist Albert Einstein lived and worked from 1933 until his death in 1955.

New Jersey's Lighthouses

The long coastline of New Jersey is dotted with great lighthouses you can visit. Some of the most famous ones are the Hereford Inlet Lighthouse in North Wildwood (built in the nineteenth century), the Cape May Lighthouse (built in 1859), Sandy Hook Light (built in 1764), Absecon Light (built in 1857), and Barnegat Light (built in 1835).

Twin Lights Lighthouse

19

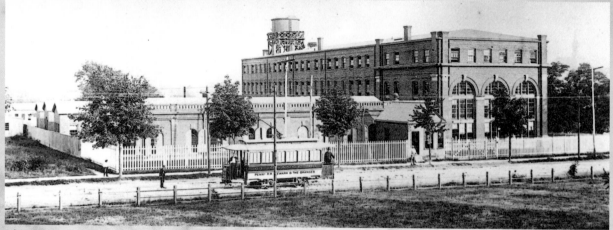

Thomas Edison's Laboratory in West Orange

Edison National Historic Site

The laboratory and home of inventor Thomas Edison are preserved in West Orange. More than half of Edison's nearly 1,100 patented inventions were researched and developed here. In addition to the lightbulb and the phonograph, he invented the first motion picture camera, an automatic telegraph system, the first sound recording, and the nickel-iron battery.

Thomas Alva Edison

Morristown National Historical Park

Created in 1933, Morristown National Historical Park preserves sites in the area of New Jersey occupied by George Washington and the Continental army during the Revolutionary War. Visitors can tour the historic Jacob Ford Mansion that served as General Washington's headquarters during the winter of 1779–1780. In the Jockey Hollow Unit of the park, visitors can see reproductions of the quarters where the Continental soldiers spent two frigid winters. The park also offers 27 miles of hiking trails.

Washington's Headquarters

The Pine Barrens

Lake Absegami

This vast wilderness in southern New Jersey covers more than 20,000 acres. It is famous for its forests of pygmy pines that grow no taller than five feet. Home to a variety of wildlife, including many rare and endangered plants and animals, the area contains many state and county parks, forests, and pristine streams and lakes.

Atsion Lake

Old Barracks Museum

Trenton

In New Jersey's state capital you can take a tour of the second-oldest capitol building in continuous use in the United States. The gold-domed State House was built in 1792. You can also visit the Old Barracks Museum, the site of the famous Battle of Trenton where General George Washington led the defeat of the Hessian soldiers. The battle is reenacted each year on the Saturday after Christmas. Historical interpreters in period clothing give tours of the barracks year-round.

Lucy the Elephant

Built in 1881 as a tourist attraction near the beach in Margate, Lucy is now a National Historic Landmark. You can take a tour inside the sixty-five-foot-high elephant and view the ocean from the very top.

Lucy

Golden dome of the State House in Trenton

Famous People from New Jersey

Edwin Eugene (Buzz) Aldrin, Jr. (1930–)

On July 20, 1969, Buzz Aldrin became the second person to walk on the moon. He was the pilot of the *Apollo 11* lunar module, the first spacecraft ever to land on the surface of the moon.

Before that, in 1966, he flew into space on *Gemini 12*. During that mission, his space walk was the longest and most successful of its time.

Judy Blume (1938–)

Born in Elizabeth, this popular author has written such children's books as *Are You There, God? It's Me, Margaret; Then Again, Maybe I Won't; Tales of a Fourth Grade Nothing; Blubber;* and *Superfudge.* She's written best-selling novels for adults, too.

Grover Cleveland (1837– 1908)

Grover Cleveland, America's twenty-second and twenty-fourth president, spent the first four years of his life living in the parsonage of the First Presbyterian Church in Caldwell, where his father was a minister.

James Fenimore Cooper (1789–1851)

This author's most famous book is *The Last of the Mohicans,* one of a series of books called "Leatherstocking Tales." Each book tells of pioneer life and features the woodsman and scout Leatherstocking (also known as Natty Bumppo or Hawkeye). Cooper's knowledge of the wilderness came from his childhood experiences in Cooperstown, NY (established by his father, William Cooper, in 1789), where Native Americans regularly came to trade.

Whitney Houston (1963–)

Whitney Houston began her singing career with a gospel choir when she was eleven years old. She is the first performer ever to have seven consecutive number-one singles on the *Billboard* magazine pop-music charts.

Paul Robeson (1898–1976),

Paul Robeson was a singer, actor, athlete, and civil rights activist. In 1915, Robeson won an academic scholarship to Rutgers University where he became the first black all-American football player. He went on to earn a law degree from Columbia University Law School, then became one of the most popular actors and concert artists of his day.

Frank Sinatra (1915–1998)

Frank Sinatra was one of the country's most popular singers and actors. Nicknamed Ol' Blue Eyes because of his intense blue stare, he started out in the big band era of the 1930s and continued to make music until his death in 1998. As a movie actor he appeared in upbeat musicals such as *On the Town* as well as in serious dramas such as *The Manchurian Candidate.*

Bruce Springsteen (1949–)

The rock mega-star Bruce Springsteen ("The Boss") is the epitome of New Jersey pride. In 1972, he named his first album *Greetings from Asbury Park* after the town where he got his start.

Meryl Streep (1949–)

In *Music of the Heart*, actress Meryl Streep received her twelfth Academy Award nomination playing a devoted violin teacher from New Jersey. Famous for her skill in learning foreign and regional accents, Streep claimed she was easily able to recall the speech patterns from her native New Jersey. She didn't win an award for that role, but she already has two other Academy Awards — one for *Kramer vs. Kramer*, and one for *Sophie's Choice.*

John Travolta (1954–)

Some know him as Danny Zucko in the musical *Grease,* but John Travolta started his career as Vinnie Barbarino in hit 1970s TV comedy *Welcome Back, Kotter.* He made his reputation as a dancer in the 1977 movie *Saturday Night Fever.* Since then he's acted in a variety of movies from comedies and action thrillers to serious dramas.

Stephen Crane's *The Red Badge of Courage*

Stephen Crane was born in Newark, New Jersey, in 1871. At the age of twenty, he moved to New York City to begin a career as a writer. He worked as a freelance reporter in some of the poorest neighborhoods in the city, writing about the harsh conditions he witnessed.

In 1895, at the age of twenty-four, he became famous when his novel *The Red Badge of Courage* was published. The book tells the story of a young Union soldier's experiences during the Civil War (1861–1865). Although Crane was born after the war ended, he seemed to have special insight into wartime suffering. His work was so convincing that he soon found work as a foreign correspondent. He was shipwrecked while on a trip from the United States to Cuba in 1896. The difficulties he suffered while shipwrecked brought on tuberculosis, which eventually caused his death, in England in 1900, at the age of twenty-nine.

The following excerpt is from Chapter Nine of *The Red Badge of Courage*. In it, the book's hero, Henry Fleming, is returning from battle with his regiment. He feels guilty because he hasn't been wounded like so many others around him, including one badly injured man he calls "the spectral [meaning ghostlike] soldier." At the end of the passage Henry discovers the soldier is an old friend.

. . . he was amid wounds. The mob of men was bleeding. . . . He now felt that his shame could be viewed. He was continually casting sidelong glances to see if the men were contemplating the letters of guilt he felt burned into his brow.

At times, he regarded the wounded soldiers in an envious way. He conceived persons with torn bodies to be peculiarly happy. He wished that he, too, had a wound, a red badge of courage.

The spectral soldier was at his side like a stalking reproach. The man's eyes were fixed in a state into the unknown. His gray, appalling face had attracted attention in the crowd, and men, slowing to his dreary pace, were walking with him. They were discussing his plight, questioning him and giving him advice. In a dogged way he repelled them, signing to them to go on and leave him alone. The shadows of his face were deepening and his tight lips seemed holding in check the moan of great despair. . . . As he went on, he seemed always looking for a place, like one who goes to choose a grave.

Something in the gesture of the man as he waved the bloody and pitying soldiers away made the youth start as if bitten. He yelled in horror. Tottering forward he laid a quivering hand upon the man's arm. As the latter slowly turned his waxlike features toward him, the youth screamed: "Gawd! Jim Conklin!"

Alfred Joyce Kilmer — Poet of New Jersey

Alfred Joyce Kilmer is more commonly known as Joyce Kilmer, the name under which he wrote. He was born in New Brunswick in 1886. During his short life (he died at age thirty-two) he worked as an editor for *The New York Times* and also wrote a number of poems. The most famous of his poems is called "Trees." A special beech tree in Mahwah, one of the towns he lived in, has been designated the Joyce Kilmer Tree.

Trees

By Joyce Kilmer

I think that I shall never see
A poem lovely as a tree
A tree whose hungry mouth is pressed
Against the earth's sweet flowing breast;
A tree that looks at God all day,
And lifts her leafy arms to pray;
A tree that may in summer wear
A nest of robins in her hair;
Upon whose bosom snow has lain;
Who intimately lives with rain.
Poems are made by fools like me,
But only God can make a tree.

pping Fun from the Cornfields of New Jersey

One of the surest signs of summer for people in the Northeast is sweet summer Jersey corn. You don't have to wait for the summer corn crop to prepare yummy popcorn, though. You can pop it all year long. Here's how to make warm popcorn extra special.

6 cups of popped popcorn
4 tablespoons of butter or margarine
¼ cup of Parmesan cheese
⅛ teaspoon of salt

Ask an adult to help you melt the butter or margarine in a saucepan. Stir in the Parmesan cheese and the salt. Put the popcorn in a big bowl. Pour in the butter-and-cheese mixture and mix well. Enjoy!